my **revisi⏻n** notes

Edexcel GCSE (9–1) History

ANGLO-SAXON AND NORMAN ENGLAND

c.1060–88

John Wright

HODDER
EDUCATION
AN HACHETTE UK COMPANY

For James, Stephen and Rachel who have taught me so much.

The Publishers would like to thank the following for permission to reproduce copyright material.

Acknowledgements: mark schemes reproduced by kind permission of Pearson Education Ltd

Every effort has been made to trace all copyright holders, but if any have been inadvertently overlooked, the Publishers will be pleased to make the necessary arrangements at the first opportunity.

Although every effort has been made to ensure that website addresses are correct at time of going to press, Hodder Education cannot be held responsible for the content of any website mentioned in this book. It is sometimes possible to find a relocated web page by typing in the address of the home page for a website in the URL window of your browser.

Hachette UK's policy is to use papers that are natural, renewable and recyclable products and made from wood grown in sustainable forests. The logging and manufacturing processes are expected to conform to the environmental regulations of the country of origin.

Orders: please contact Bookpoint Ltd, 130 Milton Park, Abingdon, Oxon OX14 4SE.
Telephone: +44 (0)1235 827720. Fax: +44 (0)1235 400454. Email education@bookpoint.co.uk
Lines are open from 9 a.m. to 5 p.m., Monday to Saturday, with a 24-hour message answering service. You can also order through our website: www.hoddereducation.co.uk

ISBN: 978 1 5104 0322 2

© 2017 John Wright

First published in 2017 by
Hodder Education
An Hachette UK Company
Carmelite House, 50 Victoria Embankment
London EC4Y 0DZ

www.hoddereducation.co.uk

Impression number   10 9 8 7 6 5 4 3 2 1
Year   2021 2020 2019 2018 2017

Cover photo © Gang Liu/Shutterstock
Illustrations by Gray Publishing
Produced and typeset in Bembo by Gray Publishing, Tunbridge Wells, Kent
Printed in Spain

A catalogue record for this title is available from the British Library.

How to get the most out of this book

This book will help you revise for the Option B1: Anglo-Saxon and Norman England, c.1060–88.

Use the revision planner on pages 2–3 to track your progress, topic by topic. Tick each box when you have:

1 revised and understood each topic
2 completed the activities
3 checked your answers online.

The content in the book is organised into a series of double-page spreads which cover the content in the specification. The left-hand page on each spread has the key content for each topic, and the right-hand page has one or two activities to help you with exam skills or learn the knowledge you need. Answers to these activities can be found on pages 40–47.

At the end of the book is an exam focus section (pages 32–37) which gives you guidance on how to answer each exam question type.

There are a variety of **activities** for you to complete related to the content on the left-hand page. Some are based on **exam-style questions** which aim to consolidate your revision and practise your exam skills. Others are **revision tasks** to make sure that you have understood every topic and to help you record the key information about each topic.

Tick to track your progress as you revise each element of the key content.

Content for each topic is on the left-hand page.

Key terms and **Key individuals** are highlighted in the section colour the first time they appear, with an explanation nearby in the margin. As you work through this book, highlight other key ideas and add your own notes. Make this *your* book.

Shorter **revision tasks** help you remember key points of content.

Throughout the book there are **exam tips** that remind you of key points that will help you in the exam.

Contents and revision planner

Edward the Confessor ruled England from 1042 until his death in January 1066. His last years as king were shaped by the need to acknowledge a successor, eventually culminating in the invasion of England by William of Normandy.

1 Anglo-Saxon society

The roles of the king and his close advisers in **Anglo-Saxon England** were clear. Society was hierarchical and all sections knew their positions. However, the question of **King Edward**'s successor caused several nobles to put forward claims and 1066 became a year of invasions and battles.

1.1 Monarchy, government and the social system

The structure of society in England was hierarchical and this was also seen in the way that the country was governed. Each group in society knew its place and obeyed those who were above them in the hierarchy.

The role of the king and nobles

- The king was the head of the government and made all the important decisions.
- The king had to display good military skills and also ensure that laws were made and obeyed.
- He had to manage his nobles by cooperating with them and controlling them.
- The earls were the most important of the nobles. There were about six of them and they were always powerful landowners.
- If the king needed to ask for advice, he would call the Witan – literally meaning 'a meeting of wise men'.
- The Witan comprised the most powerful nobles and they offered the king their views.
- The Witan could make a recommendation if the king wanted advice on the succession.

The earls and thegns

- The earls controlled large areas of England. The most important earldoms were Wessex, Mercia, Northumbria and East Anglia.
- The earls governed their areas for the king and prevented rebellions, upheld the law and raised armies.
- The thegns were nobles who held their lands directly from the king in return for military service in time of war. They were less powerful than the earls.
- To ensure good government in the earldoms, land had been divided into **shires** and **hundreds**.
- The shires were looked after by **sheriffs** and hundreds were looked after by **reeves**.

Ceorls, peasants and slaves

- Ceorls were free men who owned their land. They had to serve in an army if called on to do so.
- Peasants rented land from the thegn and had to work on his land for three days each week.
- About ten per cent of the 2 million population were slaves and they were not free. They had no land, and worked for the thegn as farm labourers or servants.

> **Key individual**
>
> **King Edward** Edward the Confessor, King of England 1042–66

> **Key terms**
>
> **Anglo-Saxon England** The period of the history of the part of Britain that became known as England from the fifth century until the Norman Conquest of England in 1066
>
> **Hundred** A subdivision of a shire, having its own court
>
> **Reeve** A local official, in particular the chief law officer of a town or district in Anglo-Saxon England
>
> **Sheriff** The chief officer of the Crown in a shire, having various administrative and judicial functions
>
> **Shire** A county area in England

> **Exam tip**
>
> You need to know how society was organised and how each section fitted into its hierarchy. You must know the specific names and terms within each section.

How important

Complete the table below. Explain the importance of each of the following in society and government at the time of King Edward the Confessor. Give a brief explanation for each choice.

	Key features	Important	Quite important
Earls	landowners, held law and military power	important as they made the witan and were the kings closest advisors, they also controlled most land	—
Nobles	landowners, controlled mint, law, tax, military	very important – 'chosen by god' had most land and power	—
Thegns	5 hides or more landowners serve military service	—	provided military since but only really had power over peasants
Ceorls	free farmers – had to serve military time	—	as important for military and owned their own land
The Witan	Earls, advisors, landowners	kings advisors made important choices and chose the king	—

 ## Spot the mistakes

Below is a paragraph which is part of an answer to the question below. However, the candidate has made a series of factual mistakes. Once you have identified the mistakes, rewrite the answer.

Describe two features of the role of the king in Anglo-Saxon England.

One feature is that the king only made a few decisions. He had to rely on the Witan for all major decisions.

The king had to be a good military leader and so he always had an army ready. He made sure his ceorls were good military leaders too.

One feature of the king is that he made many descisions, helped with the witan for major descisions.
The king had to be a good military leader, and he could call up his army (the fyrd) whenever he wanted. He made sure his earls and thegns were good military leaders too.

One feature of the king is that he controlled the money of the country, he controlled the mint, and had his royal seal printed on all coins, as well as contolling taxes and laws regarding money.
The king was also a strong military leader, and controlled the fyrd, which was his army he could call up at any time. The fyrd was made of peasants and ceorls, and had to provide military service. The king made important military decisions with the help of the witan, and was seen as a strong and important figure in war as it was seen that the king had a special connection with god and was 'chosen by god'

1 Anglo-Saxon Society (cont.)

1.2 The legal system

- People followed the king's laws but some local legal customs still existed, such as the **blood feud**. The blood feud meant that in the case of a murder or severe wrongdoing there could be **retaliation** without resort to the courts. If the retaliation went on for too long, the king would have to intervene.
- The **wergild** was used to compensate victims of crime. The amount of compensation depended on the rank of the person in society – the higher the rank, the higher the compensation.
- Capital punishment was used for those who committed treason, or betrayed their lord or the ruler.
- Crimes against the Church could mean **mutilation**, and reoffenders also suffered mutilation.
- There were no police forces. Local communities used the **tithing** system – men were placed in groups of ten and were expected to be responsible for each other's behaviour. Anyone breaking the law would have to be brought to court – failure to do so resulted in a fine for the group.

Trials

- There were two types of courts – shire and hundred.
- Shire and hundred courts used a jury made up of people who knew both parties in the case. The jury listened to the evidence and came to a judgment.
- If the two courts could not come to a final decision, then **trial by ordeal** followed. This took place in a church.

1.3 The economy

Village and town economies

- Villages had a subsistence economy: they produced enough food for themselves and some were able to produce other materials for themselves.
- Some goods would be traded at local markets and either **bartered** or sold.
- Towns would have weekly markets where goods were bartered and/or sold.
- Craftsmen would trade their hand-made goods.
- Towns with mints would make silver coins, overseen by a royal official.

1.4 The organisation and influence of the Church

- The Church held sway over all classes in society and all people attended church.
- It was hierarchically organised, like society. There were two archbishops (Canterbury and York), fifteen bishops and numerous priests. Bishops were in charge of a **diocese** and they ensured that priests carried out their duties effectively.
- The Church owned 25 per cent of the land in England. Senior members of the Church were often members of the Witan and were advisers to the king.
- People accepted that God controlled harvests, diseases and entry to heaven. Hence, the Church was a major part of daily life.
- There were several Holy Days and many saints' days, which meant that all people could attend church services.
- There were many abbeys where monks and nuns lived. Here, the inhabitants spent time praying, writing manuscripts and growing produce.

Key terms

Barter Exchange of goods for other goods without using money

Blood feud A lengthy conflict between families involving a cycle of retaliatory killings

Diocese An area administered by a bishop

Mutilation Injuring or disfiguring severely, especially by cutting off body parts

Retaliation The action of harming someone because they have harmed you

Tithing A grouping of men, originally ten in number, for legal and security purposes

Trial by ordeal A method of determining a person's guilt or innocence by subjecting the accused person to dangerous or painful tests believed to be under the control of God

Wergild The cash value of someone's life in Anglo-Saxon England

---

Exam tip

You need to know how the legal system operated. In addition, an understanding of the economy and Church organisation is important. You will need to understand how the Church fitted into the hierarchy of society.

Quick quizzes at **www.hoddereducation.co.uk/myrevisionnotes**

Develop the detail

Below is an exam-style question. You are awarded 1 mark for identifying one feature up to a maximum of two features. The second mark is given for adding supporting information.

Describe two features of the system of trials in Anglo-Saxon England.

First feature – there were shire and hundred courts.

Now add supporting information to secure the second mark.

These used a Jury made up of people who knew both parties in the case, and came to a judgement after hearing the evidence.

Second feature – sometimes courts could not make a final judgment.

Now add supporting information to secure the second mark.

Then trial by ordeal would happen, this took place in a church and involved dangerous or painful tests to determine someone's innocence, believed to be controlled by god.

 Concentric circles

In the concentric circles below, rank order the following reasons why the Church was important in society, from the most important in the middle to the least important on the outside. Explain your decisions in the box below. There might be some debate in your group about the choices.

- the Church owned much land
- church attendance
- the Church advised the king
- fear of poor harvests.

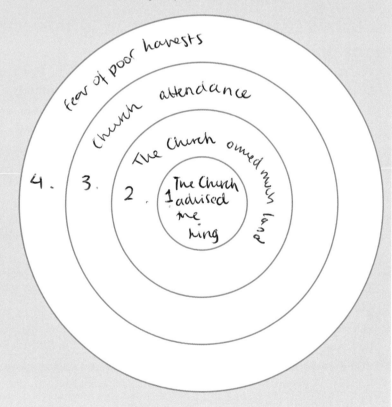

EXPLANATION

1) The Witan was made of bishops as well as earls, and made important decisions with the king, or even chose the new king.

2) The church owned ¼ of land, this meant they had much influence and power

3) All classes were expected to attend church, The church could spread ideas and beliefs through the masses, and the whole of england

4) Many went to church in fear of being punished by god (eg poor harvests) so worshipped god to have a good life.

2 Edward the Confessor and the succession crisis

2.1 The House of Godwin

The Godwin family was the most powerful family in England and was even wealthier than King Edward. As earls, Harold Godwinson and his brothers controlled much of the country by the early 1060s. Harold had a strong claim to the throne as the leading nobleman and soon put this forward on the death of Edward.

2.2 Harold Godwinson

- On his father's death in 1053, Harold Godwinson became Earl of Wessex. His brother, Tostig, became Earl of Northumbria in 1055.
- His sister, **Edith Godwinson**, was the wife of King Edward.
- The Godwinsons held much power in the Witan.
- Harold put down rebellions in Wales for King Edward and these successes brought Harold widespread support among nobles and Church leaders.
- He made a 'Danish marriage' (no church ceremony) with **Edith Swan-neck** in 1045 and they had several children.
- Harold officially married **Edith of Mercia** around the time of the Norman invasion. It is thought that the marriage was political: it gave Harold a closer link with Mercia and would secure the support of Edith's brother, **Morcar**, Earl of Northumbria.

2.3 Harold's embassy to Normandy, Tostig's actions, the death of Edward

- The **Bayeux Tapestry** shows Harold going to Normandy in 1064 to confirm Edward's promise of the English throne to **William of Normandy**.
- When Harold was captured by Guy of Ponthieu, he was freed from captivity by William. Later, Harold rescued some of William's men in a battle.
- The tapestry shows Harold promising to help William win the throne on Edward's death. The breaking of the promise is also shown.

Tostig

- Tostig was one of Harold's brothers and became Earl of Northumbria in 1055. As earl he brought stability to his province but was eventually criticised for his **tyrannical** rule.
- In October 1065, some nobles, led by **Edwin of Mercia** and his brother Morcar, attacked Tostig and his supporters. King Edward banished Tostig, and Morcar became the new Earl of Northumbria.
- Harold Godwinson supported Morcar, his brother-in-law, and suggested that he would be more able to defend the north of England from Scottish invasion.
- Tostig saw his own brother support a rival and from this point the two brothers became sworn enemies. Tostig went into exile and with his supporters began to attack the east coast of England.

The death of Edward the Confessor

- Edward died on 5 January 1066.
- It is thought that on his deathbed Edward specified that Harold Godwinson look after the kingdom, thus giving Harold an even stronger claim to the throne.
- There were no witnesses to Edward's offer.

Key individuals

Edith Godwinson Sister of Harold and Tostig, married to King Edward

Edith of Mercia Married Harold Godwinson around the time of King Edward's death

Edith Swan-neck Harold Godwinson's first wife

Edwin of Mercia Son of the Earl of Mercia. He became Earl of Mercia in 1062

Morcar Son of the Earl of Mercia. He became Earl of Northumbria in 1065

William of Normandy The first cousin once removed of King Edward

Key terms

Bayeux Tapestry An embroidered cloth, about 70 metres long, illustrating events leading up to the Norman Conquest and made between 1066 and 1077

Chronology The arrangement of events or dates in the order of their occurrence

Tyrannical Using power in a cruel or unreasonable way

Revision task

Why does the Bayeux Tapestry show Harold Godwinson confirming Edward the Confessor's promise of the throne to William of Normandy?

Exam tip

The events leading to 1066 are complicated. Make sure you know their **chronology** thoroughly.

Understand the chronology

Place the events between 1053 and 1066 listed below in the correct chronological sequence in the timeline.

Date	Event
1053	Death of HG Father
1055	TG earl of Northumbria
1065	Edwin + morcar conflict w Tostig
1065	Tostig Exiled
1066	Death of Edward the Confessor
1066	HG king

A Edwin and Morcar in conflict with Tostig 1065

B Death of Edward the Confessor 1066

C Tostig Godwinson became Earl of Northumbria 1055

D Bayeux Tapestry shows Harold Godwinson visiting Normandy 1064

E Death of Harold Godwinson's father 1053

F Tostig exiled 1065

G Harold Godwinson became king 1066

1064
D
yeux
pesity

Eliminate irrelevance

Below is an exam-style question and part of an answer. Some parts of the answer are not relevant to the question. Identify these and draw a line through the information that is irrelevant, justifying your deletions in the margin.

Describe two features of Harold Godwinson's attempts to secure his claim to the throne after Edward.

> One feature was that he was a major landowner and this made him rich. He wanted to show he was a good military leader. He put down revolts in Wales and won the praise of King Edward. This improved his standing. His brother was Earl of Northumbria and Harold was married to Edith.
>
> A second feature was that he was not on good terms with his brother Tostig. Harold strengthened his claim by offering support to Morcar when he became Earl of Northumbria and married Morcar's sister and the marriage gave him even more influence in England.

This is not phrased right, he was a landowner which made him powerful and made it easier for him to secure his power, but this should not be a key point, especially the rich part isn't really relevant.

And... explain effects and why this gave him power

Irrelevant, but could be relevant if explained that the people of Northumbria were unhappy + would welcome a new leader.

3 The rival claimants for the throne

Succeeding to the throne of England was not simply based on being a blood relative of the king. A claimant could be nominated by the king or be accepted by the nobles. A claimant was expected to be able to defend the **realm**, be an adult and be acknowledged by other leaders not only in his own land but also abroad.

3.1 William of Normandy, Hardrada and Edgar

William of Normandy

- William said that Edward had promised him the throne in 1051 and that Harold Godwinson had confirmed the promise on his visit in 1064.
- William said that Harold had promised he would help him secure the throne when Edward died.
- On hearing of Harold's coronation, William claimed it was not legal because Harold had been crowned by Archbishop **Stigand**. Stigand had been declared corrupt by Pope Alexander.
- William had proved himself a strong ruler of Normandy.

Harald Hardrada

- **Harald Hardrada**'s claim to the throne of England stemmed from an agreement made in 1042.
- Harald wanted to acquire more land and England was a rich country.
- He was encouraged to claim the throne by Tostig.

Edgar Aethling

- **Edgar Aethling** was only fourteen in 1066 and few earls supported him, despite his blood claim.
- After the death of Harold at Hastings, the Witan chose Edgar as his successor.

3.2 The Witan and the reign of Harold Godwinson

- Harold was the strongest English claimant.
- The Witan chose Harold to succeed Edward and Harold was crowned in Westminster Abbey on 6 January 1066.
- There seemed to be some haste in crowning Harold – on the day after Edward's death – and some historians believe Harold acted swiftly to deter other claimants and grant himself legitimacy.
- On hearing of Harold's **accession** to the throne, William of Normandy began making his plans for invasion. In his mind, Harold had broken his promise to help his claim to Edward's throne.
- Harold went to the north to deal with his opponents there.
- Harold married Edith, sister of earls Edwin and Morcar. This cemented his position as king and secured alliances with the two powerful earls.
- Tostig began attacking the east and south-east coasts of England.
- Harold had gathered forces to guard against invasions by William and Tostig but disbanded many of them in early September so that the men could return home and help with the harvest.

3.3 The Battles of Gate Fulford and Stamford Bridge

- Harald Hardrada and Tostig sailed up the River Humber and then the Ouse, camping outside York.
- They defeated the forces of Edwin and Morcar at the battle of Gate Fulford on 20 September.

Key terms

Accession Coming to the throne

Laying waste Destroying completely

Realm A kingdom

Key individuals

Edgar Aethling Great-nephew of King Edward. The word Aethling means throneworthy

Harald Hardrada King of Norway 1046–66. He was related to King Cnut, who had ruled England 1016–35

Stigand Leading Anglo-Saxon cleric. He was Archbishop of Canterbury 1052–70

Exam tip

Understanding the chronology of 1066 is crucial and the sequence of events must be known.

Quick quizzes at **www.hoddereducation.co.uk/myrevisionnotes**

- The victorious forces then moved a few miles south-east to Stamford Bridge to meet the army of King Harold.
- Harold had to gather his forces and march from the south coast because he had been expecting William of Normandy to invade.
- Harold and his army marched about 200 miles in five days and met Hardrada's forces at Stamford Bridge on 25 September.
- Harold defeated Tostig and Hardrada. Both men were killed and Harold removed two rivals for the throne at one go.
- Shortly afterwards, Harold learned that William of Normandy had landed in the south at Pevensey and was **laying waste** large areas of land. Harold now had to take his army south again and prepare to meet William's forces.
- Hardly any of Edwin and Morcar's forces were able to move south with Harold's tired army.

Organising knowledge

Use the information on pages 8–10 to complete the table below to show the claim to Edward's throne for each of the people involved. Tick the box which applies to each claimant.

Claimant	Blood relative	Powerful landowner	Strong military leader	Promised the throne
Harald Hardrada		✓	✓	
Tostig Godwinson		✓	✓	
Harold Godwinson		✓	✓	✓
William of Normandy		✓	✓	✓
Edgar Aethling	✓			

RAG: Rate the timeline

Below are an exam-style question and a timeline. Read the question, study the timeline and, using three coloured pens, put a **red**, **amber** or **green** star next to the events to show:

Red: events and policies that have **no** relevance to the question

Amber: events and policies that have **some** relevance to the question

Green: events and policies that have **direct** relevance to the question.

You may use the following in your answer:
- Tostig
- William of Normandy

You **must** also use information of your own.

Explain why Harold Godwinson's position as ruler was threatened by September 1066.

- **January** Edward the Confessor died
- **January** The Witan chose Harold Godwinson as successor to Edward
- **January** Harold Godwinson crowned
- Stigand supported Harold
- Harold married Edith
- Harold won the support of the nobles
- Tostig attacked southern England
- Harvest was ready
- William of Normandy prepared forces
- **September** Tostig and Hardrada sailed up the Humber
- **September** Edwin and Morcar raised forces
- **September** York threatened
- **September** Tostig defeated
- **September** Hardrada killed
- **September** William landed on the south coast

1066

4 The Norman invasion

In September, Harold had decided to let many of his soldiers return to their homes to help with the harvest. It was felt that it was too late in the year now to send an invasion fleet. However, Harold was proved wrong – twice. After defeating Tostig and Harald, Harold knew he would have to face William sooner or later. He decided to march south quickly and confront William. Harold's men had little time to recover and he was unable to gather many reinforcements. The two armies met near Hastings on 14 October and after a fierce battle, William was victorious.

4.1 The Battle of Hastings

- Harold's forces were about 6000 and William's at least 7500 (some estimates place his forces as high as 15,000).
- Harold positioned his men at the top of Senlac Hill.
- The Normans were unable to break through the English shield wall.
- Eventually, some of the Normans appeared to flee, thinking William was dead. William confronted his troops, showed he was alive and rallied them. They turned and attacked the charging English.
- Gyrth and Leofwine, Harold's brothers, were killed and then Harold too. Resistance crumbled and William was the victor.

4.2 The reasons for William's victory

- William's forces were fresh and had been well provisioned during the summer.
- Harold's army had had to march well over 400 miles and fight a major battle in less than a month. Supplying them had not been easy.
- William was aware of Harold's approach.
- Harold was unable to use the forces of Edwin and Morcar.
- William's leadership skills were crucial: his speech before the battle boosted morale. His appearance and rallying call when his forces thought he was dead proved to be a turning point in the battle.
- William was adaptable and changed his tactics later in the day by allowing his three types of soldiers to attack simultaneously.
- The Normans had a variety of soldiers – archers and **crossbow** men, cavalry and infantry, who were better armed than the English.
- William was able to move among his soldiers on horseback. Harold was on foot.
- Luck was on the side of the Normans when the English decided to chase the fleeing soldiers.

> **Key term**
>
> **Crossbow** A weapon for shooting arrows, composed of a curved piece of wood with a tight cord to propel the short arrow

> **Exam tip**
>
> If asked a question about the reasons why William was successful at Hastings, be careful not to describe the battle.

How important

Copy and complete the table below.

- Briefly summarise why each factor enabled William to win the Battle of Hastings.
- Make a decision about the importance of each factor in winning the battle. Give a brief explanation for each choice.

Factor	Key features	Decisive	Important	Quite important
Harold had already fought a battle at Stamford Bridge	had to march 400m back down to Hastings		very – men were tired	
Some forces of Harold did not march south				
Use of the cavalry				
William's leadership				
Different types of soldiers on William's side				
Supplying the soldiers				
Luck				
Norman forces adaptable				
Saxon leaders killed during the battle				

 Causation

Below is an exam-style question.

Explain why William won the Battle of Hastings.

To answer the question above, you need to explain three causes. It is sensible to make use of the two given points. However, you will need to explain a third cause. You could select one of these from the table in the 'How important' activity above. Write down your choice and the reasons behind it.

> You may use the following in your answer:
> - The Battle of Stamford Bridge
> - William's leadership
>
> You must also use information of your own

Cause: Different types of soldier on williams side

Why I have chosen this cause: Because william had advantages in his army which really helped him to win te battle of Hastings

Details to support this cause: william had soldier on horseback, archer and crossbow men, his archers could go over the sheild wall and horses could give a height advantage.

Key topic 2 William I in power: securing the kingdom, 1066–87

William wanted to make an immediate impression on the English. His progress to London after his victory was slow and deliberate, showing that he intended to keep the throne. He was crowned in London on Christmas Day 1066.

1 Establishing control

REVISED

William knew that he would have to use diplomacy and military might to ensure that there was no immediate threat to his position.

1.1 Submission of the earls

- In order to show his power, William destroyed land and property on his way to London and built castles at Wallingford and Berkhamsted.
- Earls Edwin and Morcar met William and submitted to him. William allowed them to keep hold of their lands.
- If a thegn had not fought at Hastings, he could buy his land from William.
- With the Godwinson family now greatly reduced in power, William faced the remaining nobles with confidence.
- William was crowned on Christmas Day 1066. The English nobles accepted him as the rightful ruler.

William's followers

- William's friends and supporters were rewarded with land. William fitzOsbern was given much of the land held by Harold Godwinson.
- William gave land to followers who would have to pay **homage** to him and so the land would be **confiscated** if they were to rebel.

Borderlands and Marches

- Some rebellions broke out on the borders with Wales – called the Marches.
- William created three Marcher earls who built castles, and brought peace and security.

1.2 Castles

Reasons for building castles

- William built castles as soon as he won at Hastings.
- Castles enabled him to secure control of an area.
- He built castles on his borderlands and also on the coast – with the intention of repelling invaders.
- Castles showed his determination not to surrender his kingdom.

Key features of castles

- William built motte and bailey castles: these were mounds with a wooden tower – both the mound and tower gave commanding views of the surrounding area.
- The bailey was an enclosed courtyard which was fenced off and had a ditch in front of it, making attack very difficult.
- The soldiers lived in the bailey. Here the horses also stayed and food was stored.
- Eventually, stone replaced the original wood.

> **Key terms**
>
> **Confiscate** To seize someone's property with authority
>
> **Homage** A noble's acceptance of the king as his lord. The noble would make his acceptance in public by kneeling before the king and offering his hands in surrender

> **Revision task**
>
> Why do you think William chose to be crowned on Christmas Day?

> **Exam tip**
>
> If there is a question on castles, ensure that you keep the focus if it is a causation question – do not drift into a description of castles.

Importance of castles

- By 1100, between 100 and 500 castles had been built all over England.
- Castles were normally built where there was an existing settlement. The Normans often had to destroy existing buildings and were therefore not concerned about the feelings of the English inhabitants.
- If there was a rebellion, the castle could be used as a base. Moreover, if rebels wanted to control an area, they would have to capture the castle and this would be difficult.

 Explain your reasons

Below is a table of suggested reasons why William's march to London was 'slow and deliberate'. Complete the table by explaining whether the reason is weak or strong.

Reason	Weak/strong
Gave William time to build some castles	Strong
Frighten the population	~~Weak~~ Strong
Gave time for the Anglo-Saxon nobles to accept William	Weak
Showed William's strength	Strong
William's men were tired	~~Strong~~ weak

 Eliminate irrelevance

1 Below is an exam-style question and part of an answer. Some parts of the answer are not relevant to the question or may be incorrect. Identify these and draw a line through the information that is irrelevant or incorrect, justifying your deletions in the margin.

Describe two features of Norman castles.

irrelevent

One feature was that at first they were built of wood ~~which was in plentiful supply.~~ A large mound called a motte would be built to allow commanding views over an area. William wanted to build castles all over and would leave key soldiers there and his Norman followers would keep control of the building.

irrelevent

A second feature of the castle was the bailey. ~~The Bayeux Tapestry shows a bailey being built.~~ Baileys varied in size and were enclosed with a ditch in front of them. Baileys had to be big to grow food in the area.

2 Now have a go at the following question by using the writing frame below.

Describe two features of William's control of the Saxon nobles.

What is the first feature I will describe? All land in England belonged to him
~~25th Dec, oath sworn in westminster to rule if people were loyal~~
Details to support this feature:
Godwinsons lost land and followers like Montgomery gained land.
What is the second feature I will describe?
Rewarding loyalty w money and land, unloyal lost land
Details to support this feature:

2 Anglo-Saxon resistance, 1068–71

William felt secure enough to return to Normandy in 1067, but by the end of the year there had been an attack on Dover Castle and some attacks on the Welsh borders. William had to return to England to repel any threats to his throne.

2.1 The revolt of Edwin and Morcar, 1068

- Both earls left William's court and gathered support against him.
- Edwin was unhappy that William had not kept his promise about marrying one of his sisters. This was a chance to become part of the Norman royal family.
- Morcar was replaced as Earl of Northumbria and was extremely unhappy about this.
- William marched north to confront Edwin and Morcar. He built castles at Warwick and Nottingham. He marched to York, **harrying** the areas through which he marched.
- Edwin and Morcar surrendered without fighting taking place.

2.2 Edgar Aethling and the rebellions in the north, 1069

- As nephew of Edward, Edgar was seen as a threat to William. William kept him at his court and so hoped to avoid succession issues.
- Edgar soon left the court and went to the north and then Scotland. He expected to gain help against William from the Scots and the Danes.
- Norman forces were attacked in Durham and a force of English rebels marched on York. Edgar left Scotland to lead this force.
- William then marched north and laid waste to the north Midlands and the north. This show of power caused Edgar to flee. William built a second castle at York.
- William faced further problems when King Swein of Denmark attacked Kent and then sailed up the Humber and Ouse to York. Edgar returned and his supporters seized control of York, killing the Norman garrison.
- William returned north and **razed** much of the land as well as York. He stayed at York.
- The English threat evaporated and the Danes returned home.

2.3 Hereward the Wake and the rebellion at Ely, 1070–1

- **Hereward the Wake** emerged as leader of the opposition to William in the area around Ely.
- Hereward's first action was attacking Peterborough Abbey and taking its valuables back to Ely.
- Morcar joined Hereward in 1071.
- The Danes gave assistance to Hereward but William was able to bribe them to return home.
- The terrain around Ely was difficult to negotiate – most of the land was **fen** and criss-crossed by rivers – and William found it difficult to attack Hereward.
- Eventually, William found a way to attack Hereward. Morcar was captured and the captured rebels were brutally punished.
- Hereward avoided capture but was never a threat after William's attack.

Key terms

Fen Flat, low-lying marshland areas of eastern England criss-crossed by small rivers and streams

Harrying Persistently carrying out attacks on an enemy and/or an enemy's territory

Razed Completely destroyed

Key individual

Hereward the Wake Led opposition to King William in the eastern part of England in the early 1070s

How important

Complete the table below.

- Briefly summarise why each was a threat to William's position after the Battle of Hastings.
- Make a decision about the importance of each threat. Give a brief explanation for each choice.

Threat	Key features	Decisive	Important	Quite important
Edwin				
Morcar				
Edgar Aethling				
Events in the north				
Hereward the Wake				

 Spot the mistakes

Below is a paragraph which is part of an answer to the question below. However, it has factual mistakes. Identify the mistakes and rewrite the paragraph.

Why did William face threats to his throne after 1066?

> You may use the following in your answer:
> - Edgar Aethling
> - Hereward the Wake
>
> You **must** also use information of your own.

One reason why William faced threats was the existence of Edgar Aethling, who was the ~~son~~ of Edward the Confessor. Edgar was a good military leader and could count on the support of all English nobles. At first Edgar stayed at William's court but soon decided to challenge him for the throne. In order to challenge William, Edgar went to Scotland and then went to Denmark to get help from the king there. Edgar's army was a threat and he attacked York but was defeated trying to capture the city.

_____
_____
_____
_____
_____
_____
_____
_____
_____
_____

3 The legacy of resistance to 1087

William grew frustrated at the attacks from the north of England and he came to the conclusion that he would have to be quite punitive, having hitherto been diplomatic and unwilling to be seen as an aggressive foreign ruler who had seized the throne.

3.1 The harrying of the north, 1069–70

- William was extremely angry about the rebellions.
- He sought revenge for those Normans who were killed.
- As a result of the rebellions, William laid waste to much of the north (Yorkshire, Durham and Northumberland) but also parts of Lancashire, Cheshire and Staffordshire.
- William thought there might be more rebellions, so he wanted to put fear into the population: houses and crops were destroyed and crops were burned.
- Much of the land between York and Durham was not farmed for many years.
- Sources of the time talk of rotting dead bodies and robbers in the area.
- William had many peasants killed – guilty as well as innocent.
- Many people in the north became refugees and fled their homes. Some went as far south as Evesham, more than 120 miles from York.
- Many villages – according to the Domesday Survey (see page 26) – were worth less in 1087 than they had been in 1066.
- William celebrated Christmas in York in 1069 and wore his crown to show the local population that he was the legitimate King of England.

3.2 Changes in land ownership, 1066–87

- In 1066, there were about 5000 thegns. By 1086, almost all had lost their lands.
- By the end of William's reign, ten barons held about 25 per cent of all the land in England.
- William owned about twice as much land as all other landowners put together.
- Of the 1000 tenants-in-chief in 1086, only thirteen were English.
- The key English earldoms of Wessex, Mercia and Northumbria were broken up by William.

3.3 Maintaining royal power

- Between 1072 and 1087, William spent only twenty per cent of his time in England and thus must have felt that his power was secure.
- Rebels were mutilated when captured.
- People were killed and villages were destroyed by William's forces as they marched to the rebellions.
- Lands were confiscated and people were stripped of their titles.
- Many castles were built. Initially, William built castles in Sussex and then on his way to London. After his coronation, his followers built castles on the land they were given. This meant that the landscape of England in the Midlands and the south was dominated by castles.
- William placed his own supporters in key religious, geographical and political positions.

> **Exam tip**
>
> Remember to consider William's reactions to events and his increasingly tougher attitude to the Anglo-Saxons.

Relevance

Below are an exam-style question and a series of statements. Decide which statements are:

- relevant to the question (R)
- partially relevant to the question (PR)
- irrelevant to the question (I).

Tick the appropriate column.

You may use the following in your answer:
- Harrying of the north
- Land ownership

You **must** also use information of your own.

Explain why William's methods of maintaining power helped him to secure his position as king.

Factor	R	PR	I
Land was confiscated from Anglo-Saxon nobles			
William was angry about the revolts			
Villages were worth less in 1087 than in 1066			
William placed his supporters in key positions			
William took revenge on people			
Peasants were killed			
People were stripped of titles			
Normans became tenants-in-chief			
William spent most of his time in Normandy			
William built motte and bailey castles			
Thegns lost land			
There were robbers in many areas of England			

 Concentric circles

In the concentric circles below, rank order the following reasons for increased control of England, from the most important in the middle to the least important on the outside. Explain your decisions. You might find there is some debate here.

- transfer of land
- destroying property and land
- castles
- killing innocent people
- breaking up the major earldoms
- creating fear in the land.

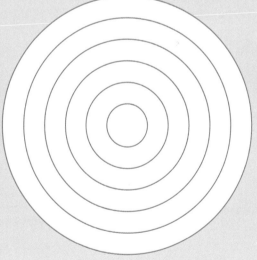

EXPLANATION

4 The revolt of the earls, 1075

REVISED

The last real threatening rebellion came in 1075. The reasons are not clear and the rebels were soon removed. The revolt is often seen as marking the end of the English resistance to William.

4.1 The reasons for and features of the revolt

The reasons for the revolt are not fully clear:

- Two powerful Norman families were to be united by marriage – the fitzOsberns and the de Gaels.
- It is thought that William did not approve of the marriage between Emma fitzOsbern and **Ralph**, Earl of Norfolk.
- **Roger fitzOsbern**, Earl of Hereford, was involved. He inherited land from his father, who had been a close friend of William. It is thought that Roger felt that he should have inherited more land and been accorded greater status by William.
- It is thought that Ralph, Earl of Norfolk, had similar complaints as fitzOsbern about William.
- **Waltheof**, Earl of Northumbria, an English earl, was also disappointed after having been given only part of the earldom.
- The earls wanted to dethrone William, who was away in Normandy. They planned to divide the country between themselves. They hoped to gain Danish support.
- Waltheof told William's regent, Archbishop Lanfranc, about the plot. Lanfranc sent two armies north and prevented the rebels' forces from joining together.
- It is not known why Waltheof told Lanfranc about the plot.

4.2 The defeat of the earls and its effects

- The revolt was very poorly planned.
- There was little support from the local populations.
- Danish forces arrived late, attacked York and plundered it and then returned home.
- Ralph and his wife went to Brittany, having fled from the forces sent by **Odo**.
- Roger had his lands confiscated and was imprisoned until his death.
- Waltheof was imprisoned and then beheaded. He was the last English earl.
- There were no more revolts after this one.

Key individuals

Odo Half-brother of King William. He was Bishop of Bayeux in Normandy

Ralph Son of one of William's chief advisers who was given large areas of land after the Battle of Hastings

Roger fitzOsbern Son of William fitzOsbern who was one of William's chief Norman supporters and was rewarded with large amounts of land after Hastings

Waltheof The last Anglo-Saxon earl. He was son of Siward, Earl of Northumbria, and was given his father's lands by William

Revision task

Draw a timeline from 1066 to 1075 showing the major events of William's reign.

Exam tip

Ensure that you learn carefully the names of the various participants.

Identifying causation

Below is a list of statements about the revolt of the earls. Identify with a tick those which are statements of causation about the revolt.

Disappointed nobles	
William out of the country	
Danish forces arrived late	
The marriage of Roger and Emma brought two powerful families together	
Archbishop Lanfranc was told about the plot	
Waltheof less powerful than Norman nobles	

 How important

Complete the table below.

- Briefly summarise why each factor contributed to the failure of the revolt of the earls.
- Make a decision about the importance of each factor in the failure of the revolt. Give a brief explanation for each choice.

Factor	Key features	Decisive	Important	Quite important
Roger of Hereford wanted more power				
Ralph of Norfolk				
Waltheof				
Danish forces failed to arrive on time				
William's refusal to allow the marriage of Emma fitzOsbern and Ralph				

Land ownership determined much of life in Norman England. William was careful to ensure that the Church, government and the law all became recognisably Norman. On his death, there was a dispute about his succession.

1 The feudal system and the Church

1.1 The feudal hierarchy

Society under the Normans was organised in a very similar way to England before 1066. The king was at the top of the **feudal system**. He owned all the land and allowed his tenants-in-chief to hold it for him.

Tenants-in-chief

- The tenants-in-chief were the major landowners in England. They would pay homage to the king – this meant they accepted the king as their lord and would make acceptance in public by kneeling before the king and offering their hands in surrender.
- In return for the land, tenants-in-chief agreed to bring knights to fight for the king.
- All of William's tenants-in-chief could raise about 4000–5000 knights. It was crucial for William to be able to raise a force such as this.
- When a tenant-in-chief died, the king would decide who would inherit the land. In most cases it would be the direct heir.
- Failure to maintain his obligations would mean that a tenant-in-chief would lose his land under the system of **forfeiture**.

Knights and villeins

- A knight had to pay homage to his lord, just like the tenant had to.
- Knights had to be prepared to fight for 40 days a year in what was called knight service.
- The land a knight held was called a fief. Knights would give some of their land to local people called **villeins**.
- Villeins would farm their own land and also that of the knight. The knight's land was called the **demesne**.
- Villeins would work two or three days on the demesne. This was called labour service.

1.2 The extent of change to English society and economy

- Towns grew up around the new castles.
- The population had to come to terms with a new landowner.
- Many villages were destroyed – in Sussex immediately after the invasion and in the north during the rebellions of 1068–72.
- The value of land dropped in those areas where there were rebellions.
- Safety and security returned after the end of the rebellions.
- Women's rights changed – women had almost equal rights in the law before 1066. After 1066, Norman law placed them subject to the rule of men.

Key terms

Demesne The land owned by the king or lord that he kept in order grow his own food and keep animals on

Feudal system The social system in England after the Norman Conquest, in which the nobility held lands from the Crown in exchange for military service, and knights were in turn tenants of the nobles, while the villeins were obliged to live on their lord's land and give him homage, labour and a share of the produce in exchange for military protection

Forfeiture Being forced to hand over land and castles to the king

Villein A peasant who was not free to move away from his lord's land

Revision task

Why was forfeiture important to King William?

- Some towns developed Norman communities, for example Nottingham and Southampton.
- Southern ports began to increase trade with Normandy and France. However, the negative aspect of the conquest was a reduction in trade with Scandinavia.
- Language began to change as Norman words were absorbed into everyday speech.
- People were still concerned about the harvest, sickness, hunger and work.

 How important

Complete the table below.

Explain the importance of each of the following in society and government in Norman England. Give a brief explanation for each choice.

Factor	Key features	Important	Quite important
Land			
Tenants-in-chief			
Paying homage			
Knight service			
Villeins			

 Organising knowledge

Use the information on page 22 to complete the table below to summarise the key changes in England after the Battle of Hastings.

Factor	Anglo-Saxon England	Norman England
Land ownership		
Language		
Women		
The king		
Trade		

1 The feudal system and the Church (cont.)

At the beginning of William's reign, the Church owned large amounts of land in England and played an extremely important part in the life of English society. The Church not only influenced the everyday life of ordinary people, but its two senior clerics (Archbishops of Canterbury and York) also acted as royal advisers. Therefore, it was important that William ensured he had some control over the Church after 1066.

1.3 The Church in society

- The Church had great power and at the end of William's reign, it owned 25 per cent of all land in England.
- People had to pay a tax to the Church: the tithe – one-tenth of everything they produced. The Church could also **levy** other taxes on the population.
- William thought that the Anglo-Saxon Church was too wealthy and that the leader in England – Archbishop Stigand – was corrupt and too concerned with wealth.

Stigand and Lanfranc

- Stigand was considered by William to be a supporter of the Anglo-Saxons.
- Stigand was criticised by William because he held a second post – as well as Archbishop of Canterbury he was Bishop of Winchester.
- He had been excommunicated by the Pope because of his **pluralism**.
- William accused Stigand of carrying out duties when not officially permitted by the Pope.
- Stigand was replaced by the Norman **cleric** Lanfranc in 1070.
- William wanted Lanfranc to bring the English Church into line with Norman Church ways.

1.4 The Normanisation and reform of the Church

- By 1087, the end of William's reign, all bishops except one were Norman. Only three abbeys had an English abbot.
- In 1072, the post of Archbishop of Canterbury was made the highest post in the Church, above York. Lanfranc's rival, Thomas, Archbishop of York, now had to swear loyalty to Lanfranc. Thomas was a supporter of William and had been his personal **chaplain**.
- Regular **synods** were held to bring in reforms.
- Lanfranc gave bishops' deputies (archdeacons) greater powers to ensure that bishops carried out reforms.
- Lanfranc tried to reduce **simony**, **nepotism** and pluralism.
- After 1075, no new priests could marry and they had to follow the idea of **celibacy**.
- Lanfranc sought to ensure that monks were well educated and that there were more monasteries. Old monasteries at Jarrow, Selby, Whitby, Durham and York were restored.
- Church courts were set up to deal with moral crimes and any priest who committed a crime was to be tried in these.
- Lanfranc built new cathedrals as well as rebuilding existing ones such as York, Winchester and Ely.
- Lanfranc removed bones and relics of English saints from their resting places, claiming there was not enough evidence to prove their saintliness.

Key terms

Celibacy The state of abstaining from marriage

Chaplain A cleric who is connected with a royal court

Cleric A member of the Church who has become an official of the Church

Excommunication The act of officially excluding someone from taking part in the sacraments and services of the Christian Church

Levy Impose a tax

Nepotism Awarding posts to relatives and friends

Pluralism Holding more than one Church post

Simony Selling Church posts

Synods Councils of bishops

Revision task

Why was Archbishop Lanfranc important to William?

- The Normans destroyed many Anglo-Saxon parish churches and built new ones. The Norman churches had the names of their own saints.
- The new parish churches were a visible reminder to all Anglo-Saxons that their country had been taken over by foreign invaders.

 ## Concentric circles

In the concentric circles below, rank order the following reasons for William wanting to control the Church, from the most important in the middle to the least important on the outside. Explain your decisions. You might find there is some debate here.

- taxation
- influence over the population
- land
- place own supporters.

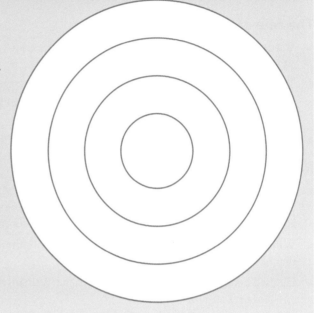

EXPLANATION

 ## Develop the detail

Below is an exam-style question. You are awarded 1 mark for identifying one feature up to a maximum of two features. The second mark is given for adding supporting information.

Describe two features of the Normanisation of the Anglo-Saxon Church.

First feature – there were Normans placed in high positions in the Church.

Now add supporting information to secure the second mark.

Second feature – the Normans set up Church courts.

Now add supporting information to secure the second mark

2 Norman government

William was keen to control as much of England as was possible. He used his senior nobles and also **regents** to assist him.

2.1 Changes to government under William

- William wanted to **centralise** all aspects of government.
- He consulted Church leaders and his earls on important issues.

The role of the earls

- William gave huge amounts of land to his closest supporters. Ten earls held about 25 per cent of the land in England.
- The earldoms were smaller than those in Edward's reign and less wealthy.
- William did not want any of his earls to be as powerful as the Godwinsons had been.
- As tenants-in-chief, the earls had to provide William with knights when needed.

Regents

- After 1072, William spent most of his time in Normandy and needed someone to take control in his absence. William spent time in Normandy defending his lands from attack by opponents including his son, Robert.
- William used regents with the same powers as him; therefore he had to ensure that he could trust his regents completely.
- He used his half-brother Odo, his close friend William fitzOsbern and Archbishop Lanfranc.
- When there was trouble, the regent was able to maintain royal authority; he had the power to raise an army.

The legal system

- William controlled the legal system and did not wish to change the English system.
- The Church became more involved in the legal system.
- The English system of tithings was continued.
- People who killed Normans were publicly executed.
- Norman-French became the court language and records were kept in Latin.
- Fines were still paid but the money went to the king, not to the victim.
- Trial by ordeal was retained and **trial by combat** was introduced.

2.2 The sheriff, the demesne and the 'forest'

- William used the sheriff as his representative in each county.
- The sheriff had to run royal lands efficiently and carried out justice in the king's courts.
- The sheriff collected taxes and fines, and raised soldiers when necessary.
- Eventually, William began to replace English sheriffs with Norman ones.

The 'forest'

- To William, the forest was any area of land he wanted to use for hunting.
- The English did not like the Norman use of land for 'forests'. (William's creation of the New Forest meant the destruction of several villages and the removal of about 2000 people.)
- There was a different legal system for the forest. Ordinary people could not hunt in the forest, cut down trees or collect wood for fuel.
- Punishment for committing these offences was usually heavy fines.

> **Key terms**
>
> **Centralise** Bring power under central control, that is, under the king
>
> **Regent** A person appointed to administer a state because the monarch is a minor or is absent
>
> **Trial by combat** A method of trying an accused person or of settling a dispute by a personal fight between the two parties involved or, in some circumstances, their permitted champions, in the presence of a judge

> **Exam tip**
>
> Ensure that you focus on how William tried to make sure that his control over England was comprehensive.

Quick quizzes at **www.hoddereducation.co.uk/myrevisionnotes**

2.3 The Domesday Book

At Christmas 1085, William ordered the Domesday Survey:

- There was a threat of invasion from Denmark and William wanted to know exactly who owned every piece of land.
- A survey would help him know how much he could raise in taxes.
- The process took less than a year and the findings were recorded in the Domesday Book.
- The Domesday Book showed how much land was worth before, during and after the Norman invasion.
- Arguing against a tax demand was now difficult because all the information was now recorded.

 Support or challenge?

Below is an exam-style question which asks how far you agree with a specific statement. Below this is a series of general statements which are relevant to the question. Using your own knowledge and the information throughout this key topic, decide whether these statements support or challenge the statement in the question and tick the appropriate box. Once you have completed this table, write an answer to this question.

'The main reason William was able to keep control of the people of England was his use of regents.' How far do you agree? Explain your answer.

You may use the following in your answer:
- Role of regents
- The legal system

You **must** also use some information of your own.

Statement	Support	Challenge
William knew there would be uprisings so he built castles		
William was in Normandy for a lot of the time so he used regents		
William used sheriffs as his representatives		
Regents could raise an army if necessary		
The law was controlled by William's representatives		
Regents were powerful landowners		
Norman-French was used in official life and thus Anglo-Saxons were at a disadvantage		
Regents were given full power by William		
Regents were William's closest allies		
William ensured that Lanfranc reformed the Church		

 Develop the detail

Below is an exam-style question. You are awarded 1 mark for identifying one feature up to a maximum of two features. The second mark is given for adding supporting information.

Describe two features of the Domesday Book.

First feature – The first feature was that William ordered the survey of England.

Now add supporting information to secure the second mark

Second feature – The second feature was that it showed who owned every piece of land in England.

Now add supporting information to secure the second mark

Key topic 3 Norman England, 1066–88

Edexcel GCSE (9–1) History Anglo-Saxon and Norman England, c.1060–88   27

3 Norman aristocracy

Norman aristocracy had many names – lords, barons, aristocrats, nobles. They brought Norman ways with them and gradually many of these became part of the way of life of the English.

3.1 The culture and language of the Norman aristocracy

- The aristocracy spoke Norman-French, though may have learned some English.
- Norman-French words were gradually absorbed into the Anglo-Saxon language.
- Norman-French became the language of teaching and of those high up in the social hierarchy. The imposition of Norman-French was another symbol of Norman superiority.
- The Domesday Book (see page 26) was written in Norman-Latin.
- The official written language of government and the Church was Latin.
- The nobles liked to show off their wealth, to display their position in society.
- Good food and clothing were symbols of their wealth.
- Their favourite pastimes were hunting and gambling.
- They had a code of honour and liked to display bravery and loyalty at all times.
- They were generous to their knights.
- Some Norman nobles learned to read and write.
- Children of the wealthy were taught at cathedral schools or in monasteries. There they learned Latin, music, mathematics, law, music and verse. Some girls received a basic education.
- Children of the Norman nobility were taught good manners and the boys learned to ride and hunt from an early age.

3.2 Bishop Odo

- Odo was William's half-brother. William made him Bishop of Bayeux when Odo was about nineteen years old.
- Odo financed about 100 ships for William's invasion of England in 1066. Odo fought at the Battle of Hastings.
- William gave Odo large areas of land in England after the invasion. Only William held more land than Odo. Odo was England's richest tenant-in-chief.
- He was made Earl of Kent in 1067 and ruled the county tyrannically. William gave him the task of keeping the south-east safe and secure.
- Odo was made regent on several occasions and sometimes shared the position with Lanfranc.
- As regent he helped to put down the revolt of the earls in 1075.
- Odo's forces attacked Northumbria after the Bishop of Durham was murdered.
- He planned a military expedition to Italy in 1082, possibly to stake his claim for the **papacy**.
- Odo refused William's request to return to England and was eventually taken prisoner by William and imprisoned until 1087. William showed mercy and, on his deathbed, decided to release Odo.
- In 1088, Odo was a key figure in the rebellion against Rufus, William's successor. Odo was supported by many nobles who held land in Normandy and England.
- Rufus was able to avert the threat by making promises to the nobles. Odo was exiled and **disinherited**.

Key terms

Disinherit To prevent an heir receiving money, property or a title at the death of the previous holder

Papacy The office of the Pope

Revision task

- Why do you think that Latin was used so widely?
- What were the main changes to the legal system made by the Normans?

Exam tip

Be careful with any dates if there is a question about Odo.

You're the examiner

1   Below are an exam-style question, a mark scheme and a paragraph written in answer to the question. Read the answer and the mark scheme and decide what mark you would give the answer.

Describe two features of the language of the Norman aristocracy.

Mark scheme	
Marks	
4	One mark for each valid feature identified up to a maximum of two features. The second mark awarded for supporting information

STUDENT ANSWER

The first feature is that the Norman aristocracy spoke Norman-French.

The second feature is that teaching in schools was in Norman-French.

Mark ☐   Reason _____

_____

2   Now write an answer that could gain 4 marks.

_____

_____

_____

_____

Focusing on the question

Below is an exam-style question.

Explain why Odo was important in Norman England in the years 1066–88.

It is important that you make it clear in your answer that you are focusing on the question. Look at the paragraph below, which is part of an answer to the question.

You may use the following in your answer:
- The Battle of Hastings
- Regent

You must also use information of your own.

One important reason for the importance of Odo was that he helped William prepare for the invasion of England. His contribution of ships greatly assisted William in moving his forces. Moreover, the contribution was important for William because it saved him great expense. In addition, Odo's presence at Hastings as a leading Norman encouraged others to help William and also guaranteed Odo's status during William's reign.

> The wording of the question is used.

> The information about Odo's provision of ships focuses on contributing to William's victory.

Now write another paragraph in answer to the question.

4 William I and his sons

William's three surviving sons – Robert, William Rufus and Henry – all expected a large inheritance when their father died. William fell out with Robert, but was eventually reconciled. William divided his land between Robert and William Rufus. England was given to William Rufus and Normandy to Robert. Despite this, there was a dispute over the throne of England, even after William Rufus had been crowned king.

4.1 The character and personality of William I

- William was physically dominating, determined and strong-willed.
- He was brave, and possessed the ability to inspire those around him.
- He was also clever, religious and politically astute.

4.2 Robert and the revolt in Normandy, 1077–80

- When William invaded England in 1066, he made his eldest son, Robert, his heir.
- In the 1070s, William allowed **Mathilda** to control Normandy, angering Robert.
- Robert demanded land in Normandy, but William refused.
- In 1079, after a family dispute with his brothers, Robert was reprimanded by William.
- Robert tried to seize his father's castle at Rouen but failed – his revolt had begun.
- Robert began attacking other places in Normandy. William attacked Robert at his stronghold of Gerberoi.
- William was defeated and was injured with his son, William Rufus.
- William was angered when he discovered that his wife had helped to finance Robert.
- His defeat at Gerberoi made William look weak. He then faced an invasion by the Scots.

> **Key individual**
>
> **Mathilda** Wife of King William I

The end of the revolt

- Robert was supported by the sons of senior noblemen.
- William was prepared to continue fighting, but was advised to make peace.
- Peace was made in 1080, and William made Robert his heir in Normandy.
- Robert led William's forces against the Scots and defeated them.
- Robert ordered the building of a large new castle to defend the border with Scotland.

4.3 William I's death and the succession

- William died in 1087.
- William had decided to leave England to his third son, William Rufus. Rufus went to England and was crowned by Archbishop Lanfranc.
- Robert and William Rufus were rivals and their supporters felt that their father should not have divided his lands.
- William's fourth son, Henry, was given money as his inheritance.

> **Revision task**
>
> Draw a timeline from 1064 to 1088 and place on it what you consider to be the ten most important events of this period.

> **Exam tip**
>
> There are many names again, so ensure that they are clearly known.

4.4 The defeat of Robert and Odo

- The division of William's land between two of his sons meant that some Norman nobles had two lords because they held land in both areas. They would have to pay homage to two masters and thus fight for each one.

- Bishop Odo supported Robert. Odo thought that Robert could unite England and Normandy.

- Odo stated that Robert would be a better ruler of England and Normandy.

- There were rebellions in England in 1088 and William Rufus attacked Odo at Rochester Castle.

- Robert did not invade England.

- The rebellions faded away. Odo was exiled and William Rufus secured his throne.

 Spot the mistakes

Explain why there were challenges to William I when he was deciding his succession.

Below is a paragraph which is part of an answer to the question above. However, it has factual mistakes. Identify the mistakes and rewrite the paragraph.

You may use the following in your answer:
- Land
- Robert

You must also use information of your own.

> One reason why there were challenges to William was because he wanted to divide England. His son William Rufus wanted Normandy and his mother helped him. He made an early claim and attacked his father. In the rebellion, William Rufus was injured and so was his father but they made peace. William I decided to split his land between two of his sons and gave England to Robert, who really wanted the lands in Normandy.

 Choosing a third cause

To answer the question in the 'Spot the mistakes' above, you need to explain three causes in order to reach a high-level mark. It is sensible to make use of the two given points. However, you will need to add one of your own. In the spaces below, write down your choice and the reasons behind it.

Reason:

Why I have chosen this reason:

Details to support this reason:

Exam focus

Your History GCSE is made up of three exams:

- Paper 1 on a thematic study and historic environment.
- Paper 2 on a British depth study and a period study, in your case Anglo-Saxon and Norman England, c.1060–88.
- Paper 3 on a modern depth study.

For the period study on Paper 2 you have to answer the following types of questions. Each requires you to demonstrate different historical skills:

- **Question 1** is a describe question. You have to describe two features of a given development or event.

- **Question 2** is a causation question. You have to write an explanation which analyses events or developments in Norman England and support your answer with precise detail. You can choose to write about the two stimuli, but you must also write about an event or development of your own.

- **Question 3** is an importance question. You are asked to make a judgement on the importance of two different events/developments, supported by a precise and developed explanation.

The table below gives a summary of the question types for Paper 2 and what you need to do.

Question number	Marks	Key words	You need to ...
1	4	Describe **two** features of ...	• Ensure you focus on a valid feature • Fully describe each feature
2	12	Explain why ... You may use the following in your answer: [two given events/developments] You **must** also use information of your own	• Analyse at least three events/developments • Fully explain each with supporting detail
3	16	'... was the most important/main/most ...' How far do you agree? Explain your answer	• Use the stimulus bullet points – failure to do so will prevent access to a higher level mark • Ensure that you introduce aspects beyond the stimulus points • Ensure that you focus on important/main/most • Fully explain its importance using precise evidence

Question 1: Describe

Below is an example exam-style describe question. It is worth 4 marks.

Describe two features of the Church in Anglo-Saxon England.

How to answer

- Underline key points in the question. This will ensure that you focus sharply on what is required.
- Identify two features of the Church in Anglo-Saxon England.
- Begin each paragraph by stating: 'One feature of the Church in Anglo-Saxon England was ... .'

- Then add some supporting information which amplifies the point you have just made.
- State the second feature. For example, 'A further feature of the Church in Anglo-Saxon England was ... .
- Then add some supporting information which amplifies the point you have just made.

Below is a sample answer to another exam-style features question with comments around it.

Describe two features of the reign of Harold Godwinson.

One feature of the reign was that Harold was chosen by the Witan. This meant that he had the support of the most important people in England.

> The question is focused on by referring to the first feature.

> Additional information is given about the first feature.

A further feature was that Harold was crowned the day after the death of King Edward. He did not want other people claiming the throne.

> The question is focused on by referring to the second feature.

> Additional information is given about the second feature.

✎ You're the examiner

Below is an exam-style describe question with two answers. Which is the better answer? Give two reasons why.

Describe two features of the revolt of the earls, 1075.

ANSWER 1

The earls rebelled in 1075 and wanted to get rid of William.

Another feature was that it was not planned carefully.

ANSWER 2

One feature of the revolt was that powerful nobles were involved. They were planning to divide England between themselves.

A further feature was that the revolt failed. The failure stemmed from bad planning and Waltheof's admitting the plot to Lanfranc.

Explain your reasons behind your choice.

1 _____

_____

2 _____

_____

3 _____

_____

Question 2: Causation

Below is an example of a causation question which is worth 12 marks.

Explain why William of Normandy had secured the throne of England by the end of 1066.

> **You may use the following information in your answer:**
> - Stamford Bridge
> - The Godwinson family
>
> **You must also use information of your own.**

How to answer

- Look for the key points in the question and <u>underline them</u>.
- You can choose to write about the two points given in the question but you **must** include additional detail.

- If you write about the events in the question make sure you write about at least three events. Including three events is important because you **must** bring in detail of your own.
- Ensure that your events are in the correct chronological sequence.
- Ensure that you give detail about each of the events you write about.

Below is a sample answer to this exam-style explain question with comments around it.

William secured the throne by the end of 1066 because he was fortunate that before the Battle of Hastings, his forces were able to rest and prepare for combat after landing at Pevensey. This was in contrast to the forces of Harold which had had to march from London and engage the armies of Tostig and Harald Hardrada at Stamford Bridge. After victory there, they had to march south to face William and his army. Thus, combat and two lengthy marches had taken their toll on Harold's men, giving William a distinct advantage, and contributed to his victory at Hastings. Victory at Hastings was gained as a result of several other factors, notably the leadership of William and the way in which he used his forces. Once victory had been gained, William was careful to emphasise to the population in a clear and precise manner that he was now the rightful king and the false claimant Harold was dead.

> Using the words of the question gives immediate focus.

> There is a developed analysis of the information using precise details.

Victory at Hastings resulted in the death of not only Harold but also his brothers and this helped William to secure the throne rather more easily than he had expected. The deaths of several members of the Godwinson family – the most powerful in England – meant that it was now a shadow of its former strength and William need not fear it. A dead Harold meant that the strongest claimant to the throne was now out of the way and he could not be a focus for restoring to the Crown. William decided on a strategy to prevent any restoration – a policy of castle building.

> A link is made between the first and second points.

> There is a developed explanation of the second point.

Having won at Hastings, William secured his throne by building castles over the southern part of England and near to London – a centre of population. The castles would be visible symbols of William's power and would be a deterrent to any noble wishing to rebel. Moreover, William gave land to his Norman supporters and they began to construct castles in their areas to secure not only their property but also the Norman Conquest.

> A link between the second point and the newly introduced third point is made.

> There is a developed analysis of the point.

'Through the eyes' of the examiner

Below is an exam-style explain question with part of a sample answer. It would be useful to look at this answer 'through the eyes' of an examiner. The examiner will look for the following:

- events in the correct sequence
- clear links between events
- an explanation of each event.

You need to:

- Highlight words or phrases which show that the answer has focused on the question.
- Underline where attempts are made to show links between one event and the next.
- In the margin write a word or phrase which sums up each specific explanation as it appears.

Explain why William carried out the 'harrying of the north' in 1069–70.

> **You may use the following information in your answer.**
> - Rebellions
> - Punishment
>
> **You must also use information of your own.**

William carried out the 'harrying of the north' because of rebellions in the north and Midlands. He put down trouble in the Midlands and the north in 1068 and built several castles (Warwick, Nottingham, Lincoln). However, further trouble erupted in 1069 when the Norman garrison was killed at Durham. In addition, another rebellion started and the rebels were helped by invading Danes. William then marched north. He was concerned that the rebels and Danish allies might disappear into the countryside and live off the land. He was determined to stop the continued rebellions.

William had begun his reign by trying not to be too harsh but after several rebellions he seemed to be running out of patience. Therefore, he sought to punish the rebels and let the population know that he was unwilling to accept any further attempts to unsettle his reign. William was angry at the population and their lords and was at pains to show the nobles as well as ordinary people that he would not accept further challenges to his throne.

 ## Adding a third cause

The answer above does not include a third reason. What would you choose as a third reason and why? Try completing the answer, remembering to add details to support your chosen reason.

Exam focus

Question 3: Importance

Below is an exam-style importance question.

'The main consequence of the Norman invasion of England was the Normanisation of the Church.' How far do you agree? Explain your answer.

> You may use the following in your answer:
> - The work of Archbishop Lanfranc
> - Land ownership
>
> You **must** also use information of your own.

How to answer

- You are advised to use the two points offered in the question but above all, you **must** give some judgement on the demand of the question – it may be similarity, difference, change, continuity, causation or consequence – failure to do so will mean a low-level mark.

- Underline key points in the question. This will ensure that you focus sharply on what the question wants you to write about.
- Remember for each development that you choose, the focus of the question is judgement about the issue(s) mentioned in the first bullet point above.

Below is a part of a sample answer to this exam-style importance question with comments around it.

The Normanisation of the Church was a key consequence of the invasion of England. Normanisation was certainly very significant because it gave William even more control over his new territory. The Church was a huge landowner, collected taxes and influenced the everyday lives of ordinary people. William needed the Church to be a part of his Norman state. He was able to have his own appointment, Lanfranc, as Archbishop of Canterbury, the head of the Church. William and Lanfranc ensured that all senior positions in the Church were awarded to Normans and that these people led the Church in the Norman way. Any corruption was rooted out and a more educated clergy was demanded. The building programme of cathedrals and even parish churches indicated yet again to the Anglo-Saxons who was in charge of the country. Hence the Normanisation of the Church was crucial.

> There is an immediate focus on the key word of the question: consequence.

> A developed explanation is given using precise details.

> The consequence of Normanisation is focused on again.

You're the examiner

Below are an answer to the exam-style judgement question on page 36 and a mark scheme. It has the paragraph from above and a second paragraph.

1   Read the answer and the mark scheme. Decide which level you would award the two paragraphs. Write the level below, along with a justification for your choice.

Mark scheme

Level	Marks	
1	1–4	A simple or generalised answer is given, showing limited development, organisation of material and knowledge and understanding. There is no judgement or the judgement is asserted
2	5–8	An explanation is given is given showing some attempt to analyse importance. It shows some reasoning, but may lack organisation. Accurate and relevant information is added. Some weak judgement is offered. Top of Level 2 can only be reached if information beyond the two stimulus points is included
3	9–12	An explanation is given, showing analysis of importance, and is well structured. Accurate and relevant knowledge is included. It shows good knowledge and understanding of the required characteristics of the period. Judgement is offered with some justification. Top of Level 3 can only be reached if information beyond the two stimulus points is included
4	13–16	An explanation is given, showing analysis of importance, and is well structured. Accurate and relevant knowledge is included. It shows good knowledge and understanding of the required characteristics of the period. Judgement is clear and justified. Answers cannot reach Level 4 unless they add information beyond the two stimulus points

Level ☐   Reason _____

_____

The Normanisation of the Church was a key consequence of the invasion of England. Normanisation was certainly very significant because it gave William even more control over his new territory. The Church was a huge landowner, collected taxes and influenced the everyday lives of ordinary people. William needed the Church to be a part of his Norman state. He was able to have his own appointment, Lanfranc, as Archbishop of Canterbury, the head of the Church. William and Lanfranc ensured that all senior positions in the Church were awarded to Normans and that these people led the Church in the Norman way. Any corruption was rooted out and a more educated clergy was demanded. The building programme of cathedrals and even parish churches indicated yet again to the Anglo-Saxons who was in charge of the country. Hence the Normanisation of the Church was crucial.

However, the change in the ownership of land was just a very important consequence after 1066 because it meant that William gave his closest allies large amounts of territory and they were to control these on behalf of William. It also meant that he did not have to fear Anglo-Saxon nobles and that he could expect his own nobles to provide soldiers in the event of a rebellion. Once again this meant greater control of the people of England.

2   Now suggest what the student has to do to achieve a higher level.

_____

_____

3   Try and rewrite the answer at a higher level.

_____

_____

Revision techniques

We all learn in different ways and if you're going to be successful in your revision you need to work out the ways that work best for you. Remember that revision doesn't have to be dull and last for hours at a time – but it is really important you do it! The highest grades are awarded to students who have consistently excellent subject knowledge and this only comes with solid revision.

Method 1: 'Brain dumps'

These are particularly useful when done every so often – it's never too early to start! Take a big piece of paper or even a whiteboard and write down everything you can remember about the topic you are revising, one of the units or even the whole History course. You could write down:

- dates
- names of key individuals
- key events
- important place names
- anything else you can remember.

Once you're satisfied you can't remember any more, use different colours to highlight or underline the words in groups. For example, when revising the Church you might choose to underline all the mentions that relate to the causes in red and to the effects in blue.

You could extend this task by comparing your brain dump with that of a friend. The next time you do it, try setting yourself a shorter time limit and see if you can write down more.

Method 2: Learning walks

Make use of your space! Write down key facts and place them around your home, where you will see them every day. Make an effort to read the facts whenever you walk past them. You might decide to put information on Anglo-Saxon resistance on the stairs, with the idea of resistance steadily developing.

Method 3: 'Distilling'

Memory studies show that we retain information better if we revisit it regularly. This means that revising the information once is not necessarily going to help it stay in your brain. Going back over the facts at intervals of less than a week leads to the highest retention of facts.

To make this process streamlined, try 'distilling' your notes. Start by reading over the notes you've completed in class or in this revision guide; two days later, read over them again, and this time write down everything you didn't remember. If you repeat this process enough you will end up with hardly any facts left to write down, because they will all be stored in your brain, ready for the exam!

Method 4: Using your downtime

There are always little pockets of time through the day which aren't much good for anything: bus journeys, queues, ad breaks in TV programmes, waiting for the bath to run and so on. If you added all these minutes up it would probably amount to quite a lot of time, which can be put to good use for revision.

Instead of having to carry around your notes, though, make use of something you carry around with you already. Most of us have a phone that can take pictures and record voice memos, or an iPod or something similar.

- Photograph key sections of this book and read over them.
- Record yourself reading information so that you can listen back over it – while you're playing football, before you go to sleep, or at any other time.

Access the quizzes that go with this book at www.hoddereducation.co.uk/myrevisionnotes

Timeline for Anglo-Saxon and Norman England, c.1060–88

1053	Harold Godwinson became Earl of Wessex
1055	Tostig Godwinson became Earl of Northumbria
1064	Harold Godwinson visited William of Normandy
1065	Tostig banished. Morcar became new Earl of Northumbria
January 1066	Death of Edward the Confessor
January 1066	Coronation of Harold Godwinson
July 1066	King Harold prepared forces in the south against invasion
July 1066	William of Normandy prepared forces for invasion of England
September 1066	Harald Hardrada of Norway invaded England
20 September 1066	Battle of Gate Fulford
21 September 1066	King Harold marched his forces north to face Hardrada
25 September 1066	Battle of Stamford Bridge
28 September 1066	William of Normandy landed at Pevensey
1 October 1066	Harold began his march south to face William
14 October 1066	Battle of Hastings
25 December 1066	William of Normandy crowned king of England in Westminster Abbey
1068	Revolt of Edwin and Morcar
1069	Rebellions in the north
1069–70	Harrying of the north
1070	Lanfranc became Archbishop of Canterbury
1070–1	Rebellion of Hereward the Wake
1075	Revolt of the earls
1077	Completion of the Bayeux Tapestry
1079–80	William I in conflict with his son Robert
December 1085	King William ordered the Domesday Survey
1086	Domesday Book completed
1087	Death of King William I
1088	Rebellions against King William II
1088	Rebellions failed. Odo exiled and disinherited

Answers

Page 5: Spot the mistakes

One feature is that the king only made a few decisions[1]. He had to rely on the Witan for all major decisions[2].

The king had to be a good military leader[3] and so he always had an army ready. He made sure his ceorls were[4] good military leaders too.

1   This is incorrect.
2   This is incorrect.
3   This is correct.
4   This is incorrect.

Sample answer

One feature is that the king made all the decisions. He was the head of the government[1].

The king had to be a good military leader. He would use his earls, thegns and ceorls for his army when the need arose[2].

1   One feature, which is amplified.
2   A second feature, which is amplified.

Page 7: Concentric circles

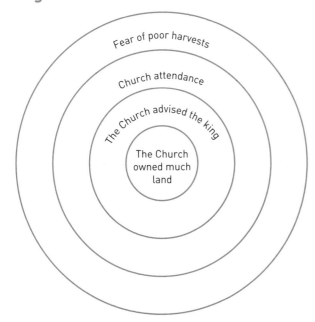

Page 9: Understand the chronology

Place the events between 1053 and 1066 listed below in the correct chronological sequence in the timeline.

Date	Event
E	Death of Harold Godwinson's father
C	Tostig Godwinson became Earl of Northumbria
D	Bayeux Tapestry shows Harold Godwinson visiting Normandy
A	Edwin and Morcar in conflict with Tostig
F	Tostig exiled
B	Death of Edward the Confessor
G	Harold Godwinson became king

Page 9: Eliminate irrelevance

~~One feature was that he was a major landowner and this made him rich~~[1]. He wanted to show he was a good military leader. He put down revolts in Wales and won the praise of King Edward. This improved his standing[2]. ~~His brother was Earl of Northumbria and Harold was married to Edith~~[3].

~~A second feature was that he was not on good terms with his brother Tostig~~[4]. Harold strengthened his claim by offering support to Morcar when he became Earl of Northumbria and married his sister and the marriage gave him even more influence in England[5].

1 Does not answer the question – not relevant.
2 Lengthy point made, which is relevant.
3 Does not focus on the question; makes a point which is not amplified.
4 Not relevant.
5 Relevant point clearly amplified.

Page 11: Organising knowledge

Claimant	Blood relative	Powerful landowner	Strong military leader	Promised the throne
Harald Hardrada			✓	
Tostig Godwinson		✓		
Harold Godwinson		✓	✓	✓
William of Normandy		✓	✓	✓
Edgar Aethling	✓			

Page 11: RAG: Rate the timeline

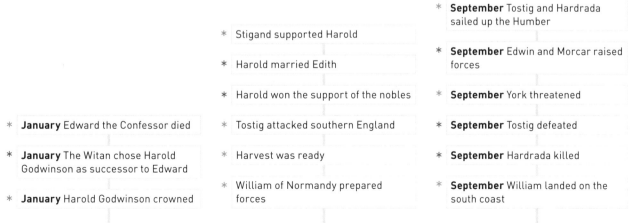

* **September** Tostig and Hardrada sailed up the Humber

* Stigand supported Harold

* Harold married Edith

* **September** Edwin and Morcar raised forces

* Harold won the support of the nobles

* **September** York threatened

* **January** Edward the Confessor died

* Tostig attacked southern England

* **September** Tostig defeated

* **January** The Witan chose Harold Godwinson as successor to Edward

* Harvest was ready

* **September** Hardrada killed

* **January** Harold Godwinson crowned

* William of Normandy prepared forces

* **September** William landed on the south coast

1066

Page 13: How important

Factor	Key features	Decisive	Important	Quite important
Harold had already fought a battle at Stamford Bridge	Harold's army had marched north and then had to march back to Hastings – there was not only fatigue but depletion of forces	Yes		
Some forces of Harold did not march south	Some went with Edwin and Morcar and others went back to gather the harvest		Yes	
Use of the cavalry	William had a more mobile army		Yes	
William's leadership	William gave a rousing speech before the battle, he had ensured his men were well-provisioned and he was visible to his men throughout the battle		Yes	
Different types of soldiers on William's side	Having different types of soldiers gave William the option to use varying tactics			Yes
Supplying the soldiers	William's forces were kept well fed. It was not easy for Harold to feed his forces on the two marches			Yes
Luck	The Saxons were taken in by the Norman feint		Yes	
Norman forces adaptable	Links to the different types of forces gave the Normans different options during the battle			Yes
Saxon leaders killed during the battle	The loss of Harold and his brothers obviously created issues for the Saxon forces		Yes	

Page 15: Explain your reasons

Reason	Weak/strong
Gave William time to build some castles	Strong – it showed the Anglo-Saxons that William meant to keep hold of his new land. The castles would secure that particular area
Frighten the population	Strong – it would frighten other people who heard about William's actions
Gave time for the Anglo-Saxon nobles to accept William	Strong – it would allow them to see that it would be difficult to oppose him
Showed William's strength	Strong – clear show of strength; destroying land, building castles; emphasising his power
William's men were tired	Weak – William was crowned on Christmas Day so his forces were recovering; local people were forced to build the castles

Page 15: Eliminate irrelevance

One feature was that at first they were built of wood which was in plentiful supply. A large mound called a motte would be built to allow commanding views over an area**[1]**. ~~William wanted to build castles all over and would leave key soldiers there and his Norman followers would keep control of the building.~~

A second feature of the castle was the bailey. ~~The Bayeux Tapestry shows a bailey being built~~**[2]**. Baileys varied in size and were enclosed with a ditch in front of them**[3]**. ~~Baileys had to be big to grow food in the area.~~**[4]**

1 Points made and described.
2 Not relevant.
3 Point made and amplified.
4 Incorrect.

Page 17: How important

Threat	Key features	Decisive	Important	Quite important
Edwin	Saxon earl who could secure help from Morcar, people in the Midlands and possibly Scotland		Yes	
Morcar	Saxon earl who could secure help from Edwin, people in the north and possibly Scotland		Yes	
Edgar Aethling	Young and a blood relation of Edward and could be a threat because of his kinship			Yes
Events in the north	General dislike of the Normans and still had links with Scandinavia		Yes	
Hereward the Wake	Local to the eastern part of England (the Fens) and not a national threat. Hereward was a continuing problem and might be a focal point for the Scandinavians			Yes

Page 17: Spot the mistakes

One reason why William faced threats was the existence of Edgar Aethling, who was the son[1] of Edward the Confessor. Edgar was a good military leader[2] and could count on the support of all English nobles[3]. At first Edgar stayed at William's court but soon decided to challenge him for the throne. In order to challenge William, Edgar went to Scotland and then went to Denmark[4] to get help from the king there. Edgar's army was a threat and he attacked York but was defeated[5] trying to capture the city.

1 Incorrect.
2 Incorrect.
3 Doubtful, perhaps some.
4 Incorrect.
5 Wrong – he captured the city but fled when William approached with an army.

Page 19: Relevance

Factor	R	PR	I
Land was confiscated from Anglo-Saxon nobles	Y		
William was angry about the revolts	Y		
Villages were worth less in 1087 than in 1066		Y	
William placed his supporters in key positions	Y		
William took revenge on people	Y		
Peasants were killed	Y		
People were stripped of titles		Y	
Normans became tenants-in-chief	Y		
William spent most of his time in Normandy			Y
William built motte and bailey castles	Y		
Thegns lost land	Y		
There were robbers in many areas of England			Y

Page 19: Concentric circles

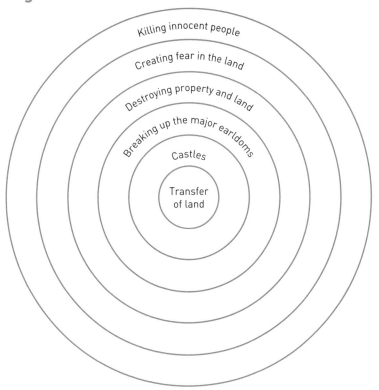

Killing innocent people

Creating fear in the land

Destroying property and land

Breaking up the major earldoms

Castles

Transfer of land

Page 21: Identifying causation

Disappointed nobles	✓
William out of the country	✓
Danish forces arrived late	✗
The marriage of Roger and Emma brought two powerful families together	✓
Lanfranc was told about the plot	✗
Waltheof less powerful than Norman nobles	✓

Page 21: How important

Factor	Key features	Decisive	Important	Quite important
Roger of Hereford wanted more power	Did not receive all his father's lands and sought greater influence with William		✓	
Ralph of Norfolk	Did not receive all his father's lands and sought greater influence with William		✓	
Waltheof	Disappointed noble – the last Saxon earl. He was involved in the plot but informed Lanfranc, thus giving William's regent time to take action	✓		
Danish forces failed to arrive on time	Danish involvement continued but their forces arrived when Ralph's forces no longer posed a threat			✓
William's refusal to allow the marriage of Emma fitzOsbern and Ralph	William did not want the marriage to take place. The marriage would unite two powerful families		✓	

Page 23: How important

Factor	Key features	Important	Quite important
Land	Extremely important – determined one's place in society	✓	
Tenants-in-chief	Vital to the king – would provide him with support if needed	✓	
Paying homage	This was the key link between the tenant-in-chief and the king. Homage was paid in public and to break trust was unthinkable. Yet, the king had to ensure that he ruled well to maintain his support	✓	
Knight service	Important for the king because this provided him with an army when the need arose	✓	
Villeins	Important because they would farm land if the knight was away on service for the king		✓

Page 23: Organising knowledge

Factor	Anglo-Saxon England	Norman England
Land ownership	About six major earls and their thegns, the king and the Church owned the land	Earldoms reduced in size and the land was held by tenants-in-chief. The king owned all the land except that of the Church, the Church owned about 25 per cent of the land, knights held land under the tenants-in-chief
Language	Anglo-Saxon was used apart from in church	Latin became the language of government. Norman became used in higher parts of society and Norman words were gradually used in everyday language
Women	In most instances, women had equal rights with men	Women in Norman law became subject to male rule
The king	The king had his own land. He made all the decisions of government but was advised by the Witan. He relied on his earls and their thegns when needed	The king owned all the land and allowed his tenants-in-chief to hold it for him. He made all his decisions but relied on some close advisers
Trade	Trade with Europe, especially close links with Scandinavia	Trade links with Normandy and France grew; trade with Scandinavia diminished

Page 25: Concentric circles

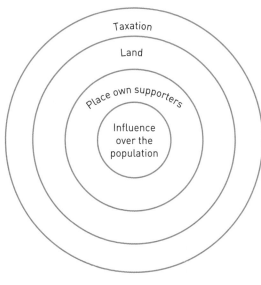

Explanation

1 The Church had influence/control over the whole population and this was competition for the king – therefore he wanted control over their whole existence.

2 If William had his own supporters running the Church then his own ideas could be transmitted to the people and control would follow.

3 The Church owned 25 per cent of the land and William saw this as a possible challenge.

4 As king he could levy taxes and he saw the Church's ability to do so as a challenge, as if it had equal or greater status.

Page 27: Support or challenge?

Statement	Support	Challenge
William knew there would be uprisings so he built castles		✔
William was in Normandy for a lot of the time so he used regents	✔	
William used sheriffs as his representatives		✔
Regents could raise an army if necessary	✔	
The law was controlled by William's representatives		✔
Regents were powerful landowners	✔	
Norman-French was used in official life and thus Anglo-Saxons were at a disadvantage		✔
Regents were given full power by William	✔	
Regents were William's closest allies	✔	
William ensured that Lanfranc reformed the Church		✔

Page 29: You're the examiner

Student answer

The first feature is that the Norman aristocracy spoke Norman-French[1].

The second feature is that teaching in schools was in Norman-French[2].

Mark | 2 |

1 One mark: valid feature identified.

2 One mark: valid feature identified.

Page 31: Spot the mistakes

One reason why there were challenges to William was because he wanted to divide England[1]. His son William Rufus[2] wanted Normandy and his mother helped him. He made an early claim and attacked his father. In the rebellion, William Rufus[3] was injured and so was his father but they made peace. William I decided to split his land between two of his sons and gave England to Robert[4], who really wanted the lands in Normandy[5].

1 Incorrect: it should read 'his lands'.

2 Incorrect: it should read 'Robert'.

3 Should read 'Robert'.

4 Should read 'William Rufus'.

5 Delete the last part.

Page 33: You're the examiner

1 Answer 2 is the better response because Answer 1 only identifies the feature.

2 Answer 2 amplifies the features in both cases.

Page 35: 'Through the eyes' of the examiner

William carried out the 'harrying of the north' because of rebellions in the north and Midlands[1]. He put down trouble in the Midlands and the north in 1068 and built several castles (Warwick, Nottingham, Lincoln). However, further trouble erupted in 1069 when[2] the Norman garrison was killed at Durham and this angered William[3]. In addition[4], another rebellion started and the rebels were helped by invading Danes. William then marched north. He was concerned that the rebels and Danish allies might disappear into the countryside and live off the land. He was determined to stop the continued rebellions[5].

William had begun his reign by trying not to be too harsh but after several rebellions he seemed to be running out of patience. Therefore, he sought to punish the rebels and let the population know that he was unwilling to accept any further attempts to unsettle his reign. William was angry at the population and their lords and was at pains to show the nobles as well as ordinary people that he would not accept further challenges[6] to his throne.

1 Focuses clearly on the question and adds detail.

2 Further detail linked.

3 Extra words added.

4 Links made.

5 Focuses on the question.

6 Clear focus on the question.

Matter And Consciousness

John Woodroffe

MATTER AND CONSCIOUSNESS [1]

ACCORDING TO THE SHĀKTA ĀGAMA

By SIR JOHN WOODROFFE

THE subject of my lecture to-day is Consciousness or Chit, and Matter or Unconsciousness, that is, Achit; the unchanging formlessness and the changing forms. According to Shākta Advaitavāda we are Consciousness-Unconsciousness or Chit-Achit; being Chit-Shakti as regards our Antarātmā and the particularised Māyā Shakti as to our material vehicles of

[1] Short summary of address delivered at the Dacca Sahitya Parishat, June, 1916

mind and body. The reason that I have selected this subject, amongst the many others on which I might have addressed you, is that these two ideas are the key concepts of Indian Philosophy and religion. If they are fully understood, both as to their definition and relations, then all is understood so far as intellect can make such matters intelligible to us; if they are not understood, then nothing is properly understood. Nor are they always understood even by those who profess to know and write on Indian Philosophy. Thus the work on Vedānta of an English Orientalist, now in its second edition, describes Chit as the condition of a stone or other inert substance. A more absurd error it is hard to imagine. Those who talk in this way have not learnt the elements of their subject. It is true that you will find in the Shāstra the state of the Yogī described as being like a log (Kāshtavat). But this does not mean that his consciousness is that of a piece of wood, but that he no more perceives the external world than a log of wood does. He does not do so because he has the Samādhi consciousness that is illumination and true Being itself.

I can to-night only scratch at the surface of a profound subject. To expound it properly would require a series of lectures, and to understand it in its depths, years of thinking thereon. I will look at the matter first from the scientific point of view; secondly state what those concepts mean in themselves; and thirdly show how they are related to one another in the Sāngkhya and the Māyāvāda and Shaktivāda presentments of Vedānta doctrine. The Shaktivāda, with which I deal to-night, may be found in the Tantras. It has been supposed that the Āgamas arose at the close of the age of the Upanishads. They are Shāstras of the Upāsanā Kānda dealing with the worship of Saguna Īshvara. It has been conjectured that they arose partly because of the declining strength of the Vaidika Āchāra and partly because of the increasing number of persons within the Hindu fold who were not competent for the Vaidika

Achāra and for whom some spiritual discipline was necessary. One common feature distinguishes them; namely, their teaching is for all castes and all women. They express the liberal principle that whilst socially differences may exist, the path of religion is open to all, and that spiritual competency and not the external signs of caste determine the position of persons on that path. Īshvara in these Āgamas is worshipped in threefold forms as Vishnu, Shiva, Devī. Therefore the Āgamas or Tantras are threefold: Vaishnava, Shaiva and Shākta, such as the Pancharātra Āgamas of the first group, the Shaiva Siddhānta (with its 28 Tantras), the Nakulisha Pāshupata and the Kashmirian Trika of the second group, and the alleged division into Kaula, Mishra, Sāmaya of the third group. I express no opinion on this last division. I merely refer to this matter in order to explain what I mean by the word Āgama. The Shaktivāda, however, which I contrast with Māyāvāda to-day, is taken from the Shākta Āgama. By Māyāvāda I mean Shangkara's exposition of Vedānta.

Now with reference to the scientific aspect of the subject I shall show you that in three main particulars modern Western physics and psychology support Indian Philosophy. Indeed Mr. Lowes Dickinson, in an acute recent analysis of the state of ideas in India, China and Japan, observes that the Indian form of religion and philosophy is that which most easily accommodates itself to modern Western science. That does not prove it is true until it is established that the conclusions of Western science to which it does conform are true. But the fact is of great importance in countering those who have thought that Eastern ideas were without rational foundation. It is of equal importance to those two classes who either believe in the ideas of India, or in the particular conclusions of science to which I refer. The three points on this head are : firstly, that physicists, by increasing their knowledge of so-called " matter," have been led to doubt its reality and have

5

dematerialised the atom and with it the entire universe which the various atoms compose. The trinity of matter, ether and electricity, out of which science has hitherto attempted to construct the world, has been reduced to a single element— the ether (which is not scientific "matter") in a state of motion. According to Sāngkhya the objective world is composed of the Bhūtas, which derive ultimately from Ākāsha. I do not say that scientific "ether" is Ākāsha, which is a concept belonging to a different train of thought. Moreover the sensible is derived from the supersensible Ākāsha Tanmātra and is not therefore an ultimate. But it is important to note the agreement in this, that both in East and West the various forms of gross matter derive from some single substance which is not "matter". Matter is *dematerialised*, and the way is made for the Indian concept of Māyā. There is a point at which the mind cannot any longer usefully work outward. Therefore after the Tanmātras the mind is turned within to discover their cause in that Egoism which, reaching forth to the world of enjoyment, produces sensorium, senses, and objects of sensation. That the mind and senses are also material has the support of some forms of Western philosophy, such as that of Herbert Spencer, for he holds that the Universe, whether physical or psychical, is a play of force which, in the case of matter, we experience as object. Mind as such is, he says, as much a "material" organ as the brain and outer sense-organs, though they are differing forms of force.

His affirmation that scientific "matter" is an appearance produced by the play of cosmic force, and that mind itself is a product of the same play, is what Sāngkhya and Vedānta hold. The way, again, is opened for the concept Māyā. Whilst, however, Spencer and the Agnostic School hold that the Reality behind these phenomena is unknowable, the Vedānta affirms that it is knowable and is Consciousness itself. This is the Self, than which nothing can be more intimately known.

Force is blind. We discover consciousness in the Universe. It is reasonable to suppose that if the first cause is of the nature of either Consciousness or Matter and not of both, it must be of the nature of the former and not of the latter. Unconsciousness or object may be conceived to modify Consciousness, but not to produce Consciousness out of its unconscious self. According to Indian ideas Spirit, which is the cause of the Universe, is pure Consciousness. This is Nishkala Shiva and, as the creator, the great Mother or Devī. The existence of pure Consciousness in the Indian sense has been decried by some thinkers in the West, where generally to its pragmatic eye Consciousness is always particular, having a particular direction and form. It assumes this particularity, however, through Māyā. We must distinguish between Consciousness as such and modes in consciousness. Consciousness is the unity behind all forms of consciousness, whether sensation, emotion, instinct, will or reason. The claim that Consciousness as such exists, can only be verified by spiritual experience. All high mystic experiences, whether in East or West, have been experiences of unity in differing forms and degrees. Even, however, in normal life, as well as in abnormal pathological states, we have occasional stretches of experience in which it becomes almost structureless. Secondly, the discovery of the subliminal consciousness aids Shāstric doctrine in so far as it shows that behind the surface consciousness of which we are ordinarily aware, there is yet another mysterious field in which all its operations grow. It is the Buddhi which here manifests. Well established occult powers and phenomena now generally accepted, such as telepathy, thought-reading, hypnotism and the like, are only explainable on hypotheses which approach more nearly Eastern doctrine than any other theory which has in modern times prevailed in the West. Thirdly, as bearing on this subject we have now the scientific recognition that from its *materia prima* all forms have evolved; that there is life in all things; and that there are no breaks in nature. There is the same matter and Consciousness throughout. There is unity of life. There is no such thing as "dead" matter. The well known experiences of Dr. Jagadish Bose establish response to stimuli in inorganic matter. What is this response but the indication of the existence of that Sattva Guna which Vedānta and Sāngkhya affirm to exist in all things, organic or inorganic. It is the play of Chit in this Sattva, so muffled in Tamas as not to be recognisable except by delicate scientific experiment, which appears as the so-called "mechanical" response. Consciousness is here veiled and imprisoned by Tamas. Inorganic matter displays it in the form of that seed or rudiment of sentiency which, enlarging into the simple pulses of feeling of the lowest degrees of organised life, at length emerges in the developed self-conscious sensations of human life. Consciousness is throughout the same. What varies is its wrappings. There is thus a progressive *release* of Consciousness from gross matter through plants and animals to man. This evolution Indian doctrine has taught in its eighty-four lakhs of previous births. According to the Hindu books plants have a dormant consciousness. The Mahābhārata says that plants can see and thus they reach the light. Such power of vision would have been ridiculed not long ago, but Professor Haberlandt, the well known botanist, has established that plants possess an organ of vision in the shape of a convex lens on the upper surface of the leaf. The animal consciousness is greater, but seems to display itself almost entirely in the satisfaction of animal wants. In man we reach the world of ideas, but these are a superstructure on consciousness and not its foundation or basis. It is in this modeless basis that the various modes of consciousness with which we are familiar in our waking and dreaming states arise.

The question then arises as to the relation of this principle of Form with Formlessness; the unconscious finite with infinite consciousness. It is noteworthy that in the Thomistic philosophy Matter, like Prakriti, is the particularising or *finitising* principle. By their definition, however, they are opposed. How then can the two be one?

Sāngkhya denies that they are one, and says they are two separate, independent principles. This Vedānta denies, for it says that there is in fact only one true Reality, though from the empirical, dualistic standpoint there seem to be two. If the question then is asked—is dualism, pluralism, or monism to be accepted?—for the Hindu the answer of Shruti is that it is the last. But apart from this the question is: Does Shruti record a true experience and is it the fact that spiritual experience is monistic or dualistic? The answer is, as we can see from history, that all high mystic experiences are experiences of unity in differing forms and degrees.

The question cannot be decided solely by discussion, but by our conclusion as to the conformity of the particular theory held with spiritual experience. But how can we reconcile the unity of pure consciousness with the plurality of unconscious forms which the world of experience gives us? Vedānta gives various intellectual interpretations, though experience alone can solve this question. Shangkara says there is only one Sadvastu, the Brahman. From a transcendental stand-point It *is* and nothing happens. There is in the state of highest experience (Paramātmā) no Īshvara, no crea-tion, no world, no Jīva, no bondage, no liberation. But empirically he must and does admit the world or Māyā, which in its seed is the cosmic Sangskāra, which is the cause of all these notions which from the highest state are rejected. But is it real or unreal? Shangkara says it is neither. It cannot be real, for then there would be two Reals. It is not unreal, for the world is an empirical fact—an experience of its kind—and it proceeds from the Power of Īshvara. In truth it is unexplainable and, as Sāyana says, more wonderful than Chit itself.

But if it is neither Sat nor Asat, then as Māyā it is not the Brahman who is Sat. Does it then exist in Pralaya, and if so how and where? How can unconsciousness exist in pure consciousness? Shangkara calls it eternal and says that in Pralaya Māyāsattā is Brahmasattā. At that time Māyā, as the power of the ideating consciousness, and the world, its thought, do not exist; and only the Brahman exists. But if so, how does the next universe arise on the assumption that there is Pralaya and that there is not with Him as Māyā the seed of the future universe? A Bīja of Māyā as Sangskāra, even though Avyakta (not present to Consciousness), is yet by its terms different from consciousness. To all such questionings Shangkara would say they are themselves the product of the Māyā of the state in which they are put. This is true, but it is possible to put the matter in a simpler way, against which there are not so many objections as may be laid against Māyāvāda.

It seems to me that Shangkara, who combats Sāngkhya, is still much influenced by its notions, and as a result of his doctrine of Māyā he has laid himself open to the charge that his doctrine is not Shuddha Advaita. His notion of Māyā retains a trace of the Sāngkhyan notion of separateness, though separateness is in fact denied. In Sāngkhya, Māyā is the real Creatrix under the illumination of Purusha. We find similar notions in Shangkara, who compares Chit to the Ayaskānta-mani, and denies all liberty of self-determination in the Brahman which, though itself unchanging, is the cause of change. Jnāna Kriyā is allowed only to Īshvara, a concept which is itself the product of Māyā. To some extent the distinctions made are perhaps a matter of words. To some extent particular notions of the Āgamas are more practical than those of Shangkara, who was a transcendentalist.

The Āgama, giving the richest content to the Divine Consciousness, does not deny to it knowledge, but in its supreme aspect any dual knowledge; spiritual experience being likened by the Brihadāranyaka Upanishad to the union of man and wife, in which duality exists as one and there is neither within nor without. It is this union which is the Divine Līlā of Shakti, who is yet all the time one with Her Lord.

The Shākta exposition appears to be both simple and clear. I can only sketch it roughly—having no time for its detail. It is first the purest Advaitavāda. What then does it say? It starts with the Shruti " Sarvam Khalvidam Brahma ". Sarvam=world; Brahman=consciousness or Sachchidānanda; therefore this world is in itself Consciousness.

But we know we are not perfect consciousness. There is an apparent unconsciousness. How then is this explained? The unmanifested Brahman before all the worlds is Nirguna Shiva—the blissful, undual consciousness. This is the static aspect of Shiva. This manifests Shakti, which is the kinetic aspect of Brahman. Shakti and Shaktimān are one; therefore Shiva manifests as Shiva-Shakti, who are one and the same. Therefore Shakti is consciousness.

But Shakti has two aspects (Murtti): *viz.*, Vidyā Shakti or Chit-Shakti, and Avidyā Shakti or Māyā-Shakti. Both, as Shakti, which is the same as Shaktimān, are in themselves conscious. But the difference is that whilst Chit-Shakti is illuminating consciousness, Māyā is a Shakti which veils consciousness to itself and by its wondrous power appears as unconscious. This Māyā-Shakti is consciousness which by its power appears as unconsciousness. This Māyā-Shakti is Triguna Shakti, that is, Shakti composed of the three Gunas. This is Kāmakalā, which is the Trigunātmakavibhūti. These Gunas are therefore at base nothing but Chit-Shakti. There is no necessity for the Māyāvādin's Chidābhāsa, that is, the reflection of conscious reality on unconscious unreality, as Māyāvāda says. All is real except in the sense that some things endure and are therefore truly real; others pass, and in that sense only are not real. All is Brahman. The Antarātmā in man is the enduring Chit-Shakti. His apparently unconscious vehicles of mind and body are Brahman as Māyā-Shakti, that is, consciousness appearing as unconsciousness by virtue of its inscrutable power. Īshvara is thus the name for Brahman as Shakti which is conjoined Chit-Shakti and Māyā-Shakti.

The Mother Devī is Īshvara considered in His feminine aspect (Īshvarī) as the Mother and Nourisher of the world. The Jīva or individual self is an Angsha or fragment of that great Shakti; the difference being that, whilst Īshvara is Māyāvin or the controller of Māyā, Jīva is subject to Māyā. The World-thinker retains His Supreme undual Consciousness even in creation, but His thought, that is, the forms created by His thinking, are bound by His Māyā, that is, the forms with which they identify themselves, until by the power of the Vidyā Shakti in them they are liberated. All is truly Sat—or Brahman. In creation Shiva extends His power, and at Pralaya withdraws it into Himself. In creation Māyā is in itself consciousness which appears as unconsciousness. Before creation it exists as consciousness.

Important practical results follow from the adoption of this view of looking at the world. The latter is the creation of Īshvara. The world is real; being unreal only in the sense that it is a shifting, passing thing, whereas Ātmā as the true Reality endures. Bondage is real, for bondage is Avidyāshakti binding consciousness. Liberation is real; for this is the grace of Vidyāshakti. We are each Centres of Power, and if we would achieve success must, according to this Shāstra, realise ourselves as such, knowing that it is Devatā which thinks and acts in and as us and that we are the Devatā. Our world enjoyment is His, and liberation is His peaceful nature. The Agamaṣ deal with the development of this Power, which is not to be thought of as something without, but as within our grasp through various forms of Shakti Sādhanā. Being in the world and working through the world, the world itself, in the words of the Kulārnava Tantra, *becomes the seat of liberation* (Mokshāyate Sangsāra). The Vīra or heroic Sādhaka does not shun the world from fear of it. But he holds it in his grasp and wrests from it its secret. Realising it at length · as Consciousness, the world of matter ceases to be an object of desire. Escaping ·from the unconscious driftings of a humanity which has not yet realised itself, He is the illumined master of himself, whether developing all his powers, or seeking liberation at his will.

John G. Woodroffe

CPSIA information can be obtained
at www.ICGtesting.com
Printed in the USA
LVIC060814170919
631236LV00001BA/6